Christmas & Win.

Black Bough Poetry

Edited by Matthew M. C. Smith

Guest Readers: Preston Smith, Polly Oliver & Erin Russell

Artist: Emma Bissonnet

www.blackboughpoetry.com

Twitter: @blackboughpoems

FB: BlackBoughpoetry

First published in print by Black Bough Poetry in 2020.

Copyright © 2020.

LEGAL NOTICE

Matthew M. C. Smith has asserted his right under Section 77 of the Copyright, Designs and Patents Act 1988 to be identified as the editor of this work. Individual contributors reserve copyright to their work. Typesetting by Matthew M. C. Smith. Artwork by Emma Bissonnet.

All rights reserved. No part of this book may be reproduced, stored in a retrieval system, or transmitted in any form, or by any means; electronic, mechanical, photocopying, without prior permission from the editor / authors. However, short extracts may be quoted on social media.

Editorial team

Preston Smith   Matthew M. C. Smith   Polly Oliver   Erin Russell

Guest Reader   *Editor*   *Guest Reader*   *Guest Reader*

Emma Bissonnet

Artist

Editorial note:

We're delighted to present to you our first winter festive edition in print. Huge thanks to Preston Smith, Polly Oliver and Erin Russell, three highly-talented poets who have greatly assisted the editorial process as Guest Readers. We are proud to feature the stunning work of Swansea-based artist Emma Bissonnet, who kindly agreed for us to feature her art, which is available for purchase online. Thanks also to *Seren Books* for allowing us to reprint two poems by Catherine Fisher.

We hope you are moved by these atmospheric poems.

Season's Greetings,

Matthew M. C. Smith
Editor - Black Bough Poetry
October 2020

Contents

Cold	Catherine Fisher	1
Extract from 'Frost'	Catherine Fisher	1
The Fox / Le Renard/ Der Fuchs	Pax Morrigan	2
Morning	Julian Brasington	3
Christmas in the South Slavic Lands /	Boris Simonovski	4
Божиќ во Јужнословенските земји		4
Diyas	Leela Soma	5
Festspiele	Ronnie Smith	5
10:13	Rafferty Wolfe	7
Lore	Laura Wainwright	7
Evergreen	Guinevere Clark	7
Ash to Dust	Ryan Norman	8
Pilgrimage	George Neame	8
Field Margins	Marcelle Newbold	9
A Bright Hearth	Matthew M. C. Smith	9
On Wondering …	Preston Smith	10
Behold, I Tell You a Mystery	E. Samples	10
A Silhouette	Paul Brookes	12
My Husband At Seven	Carole Bromley	12
Origami Winter	Merril D. Smith	13
The Ice Swim	Karen Hodgson Pryce	13
Christmas Box	Gaynor Beesley	14
Jólabókaflóð*	Jane Mackenzie	14
Figurine	Polly Oliver	15
Eve of Hope	Ann Christina Tabaka	15
Advent	Matthew M. C. Smith	17
The New Arrival	Caroline Hammond	17
Since You Asked	Lisa McCabe	18
First-foot	Alexandra McCauley	18
The Last Tree	Luanne Rice	19
Late Shift	Philip Berry	19
Sol Invictus	Sasha Saben Callaghan	20
Yuletide	Dai Fry	20
Ornaments	Lucy Whitehead	21
Christmas Eve	Sarah Connor	21
Christmas Eve	Alan Parry	22
Colours of Grief	Tracy Gaughan	22
Solstice	Megha Sood	23
Solstice Fair	Ian Richardson	23

Winter Solstice	*Marian Christie*	23
Samhain	*Nicola Heaney*	24
Christmas Gift 1978	*Ellie Rees*	24
In Winter's Path / Llwybr y Gaeaf	*Ness Owen*	25
Winter-maid (Matariki harvests)	*Ankh Spice*	25
Advent	*Jane Mackenzie*	27
Blossoming	*Lynn Valentine*	27
Christmas Party	*Lesley Williams*	27
Christmas morning	*Elizabeth Moura*	28
Boxing Day	*Rae Howells*	28
Christmas Message	*Lucy Dixcart*	29
Winter Solstice Incantation	*Kim Harvey*	29
Holidays are just small wakes that	*Conyer Clayton*	31
Moth	*Lorraine Carey*	31
The Edges	*A. A. Parr*	32
Winter, maybe	*Erin Russell*	32
Throwing Shade	*Ellie Rees*	33
The Star in the East	*Iris Anne Lewis*	33
End of the day	*Patrick Williamson*	34
Frost	*Matthew M. C. Smith*	34

Illustrations

All illustrations by Emma Bissonnet.

See page 37 for details on purchasing Emma's stunning art.

Cover - 'Fire Festival and Northern Lights'
'A Partridge in a Pear Tree'
'Winter Fox' - p. 2
'Snowy Owl' - p. 6
'The Hare and the Moon' - p. 11
'Cutty Wren and the Snow Moon' - p. 16
'Winter Visitor: Mari Lwyd' - p. 26
'Moon Moths' - p. 30
'Two Turtle Doves - p. 35
'Winter Wassail' - p. 36

Cold

I know it has fingers. Can see
the designs they scrape on the window.
There are other things I know;
how it strikes deep, stiffens the body

to a puppet, jerky, controlled.
Bells in empty towers hang with ice,
a bird skitters on silence.
Even the young look old.

Through my grey wood, over the fields,
no leaf falls, no starling rises.
It's not anarchy, more like some lost project,
a plan that died at the outset,
a fallen coin on the pavement
no one will unglove to collect.

(Extract from 'Frost')

This is an art deco winter,
all monochrome, all angles,
the streets cornered,
their edges neatly aligned
as if nuance no longer counts,
as if some deep geometric truth
has come out into the cold.

Catherine Fisher

Poems from *The Bramble King*, Seren Books, 2019.

The Fox

Snow in the woods.

At dusk, I walked alone
through the tree maze, spotted a trail
of elegant imprints by the hazel.

I did not follow it.

Le Renard

Neige dans la forêt.

Au crépuscule, je marchais seule
à travers du labyrinthe d'arbres, j'ai vu une piste
d'empreintes élégantes proche du noisetier.

Je ne l'ai pas suivie.

Der Fuchs

Schnee im Wald.

In der Abenddämmerung ging ich allein
durch das Baumlabyrinth, sah eine Spur
von eleganten Abdrücken beim Haselstrauch.

Ich folgte ihr nicht.

Pax Morrigan

Morning

We woke from the moon into hoarfrost
watched a fox as it sniffed out a small death
its footprints less muddied than words

Julian Brasington

10:13

The 10:13 yawns, stretches, shudders
as its snow-packed pistons forget their pain
and pull away, from a city winter-varnished grey,
the colour of northern stations at dawn
in Christmas rain

Rafferty Wolfe

Lore

Holly in a moon-found wood:
    unhung, unwound,
    unmade
by snow-starred card
and robin-perched plate.
Or embossed cup of blood.
Intricate between ghost-prints
of oak and bitter ivy. A king
who would be queen, cloaked
red under Saturn.

Laura Wainwright

Evergreen

Sun white,
cone-clad, ice-wed
in our garden shrine.
Circling roots with berry blood;
we dress you.

Guinevere Clark

Ash to Dust

Buried to my knees, ice-soled,
I call for Brighid to light
the dark, to shoulder my burden:

In the distance,
the Ash tree
flames to dust.

Ryan Norman

Pilgrimage

The clocks were days away from turning back.
The tips of the beech trees lining the South Downs'
chalky ridge flickered in yellow and amber,
a dwindling flame.

I press my knees to my mother's kitchen floor,
watching winter vegetables become crisp
and golden in the oven shrine, my hair
still clammy from the dripping of rain
off the damp straw eaves.

George Neame

Field Margins

A hedge hag praises the scent of the moon,
lingers at the edge of all things,
gathers poison in skirt-heavy folds,
as gloss-thick spines lick perfect blue.

She congregates the discarded precious:
feather, windfall stick, field mouse bone -
conjures protection, for all things,
journeys to places concealed by the sun.

Marcelle Newbold

Note: Hollies were frequently left uncut in hedges
to obstruct witches who were known to run along
the tops of hedges.

A Bright Hearth

After the snow was cleared, a new drift,
silent and silver, a spell in street light.
In crisp and cold, Christmas lights sparkle and through
doors, a stove is warm. In the dark of a room,
the halo-flame lights a face, the hunched figure
before a bright hearth. In crackle and smoke
images are kindled: the winter king's burning ship;
the infant Christ, star-cradled; wild-eyed Saturn
and his stumbling train and deeper, an older time:
a forest in bitter mid-winter, where drums beat and
shadows rush and run. A heavy bough of holly prickles
and berries, sweet and bloody, are trampled underfoot .

Matthew M. C. Smith

On Wondering Whether Persephone & Hades
Might Attend the First Supper

After religion class I was sure
Hephaestus had forged Christmas lights
from radioactive embers sprayed
from Apollo's chariot as he circled
the globe each December.

I was sure he had hung them
while Zeus ordered nymphs to cook
the first supper in Olympus.

I did not pass religion class.

Preston Smith

Behold, I Tell You a Mystery

Nine candles burning, drip and wane;
the long Cold Moon of folklore.
December crumples like a wish list:
bed of hay, guiding star,
child-king of the cross.
Nine bright fires on blue wax dance;
Oh death, where is thy sting?

E. Samples

A Silhouette

Winter is a silhouette.
A definition by outline,
colour bled into starkness
a flat surface
as if the world is ragged paper.

Shy the inexhaustible shy
of winter, worry away the rest.
Wear worn decay; the rest
hunkers into itself
as if afeard, afeard for itself

Paul Brookes

My Husband at Seven

Dressed as a pudding, you stand awkwardly
beside your Christmas cracker big brother
on that hospital ward where your father
has just carved a turkey no-one can stomach.
I can see the train-set in your eyes,
the tunnel you haven't had time to open,
the satsuma and bright coins in your dad's sock.
Matron holds the platter aloft, mother
to all these frail old women neatly tucked.

Carole Bromley

Origami Winter

That Christmas holiday in Philadelphia
we watched ice skaters from our hotel room,
and traveled by subway
as the snow fell--and kept falling--till we were marooned
at the Borenstein's, a rowhouse island in a sea of white.
We ate our Yuletide feast of bagels, cream cheese, and lox,
My sister remembers we did origami,
our memories now unfold these shapes
of winters' past.

Merril D. Smith

The Ice Swim

Wrapped in goose down
on a sleet-soaked bank,
he flaps his arms for heat.

In a smear of cloth, she
enters a snow-laced loch.
An Arctic wind whips

her skin to flames. She snaps
a frozen path to the prize –
a world view from the ice.

Karen Hodgson Pryce

Christmas Box

Clammy cardboard and mould
sweat into fairy lights,
two bulbs blown.

A plastic angel,
with shattered feet.

A card, de-glittered,
it's message faded,
a forgotten friend.

Gaynor Beesley

Jólabókaflód

I will give you a castle
etched deep on a rock,
an island gemmed and glittering.
A young woman, thrawn with care
and an ancient wolf
who howls no more.
We will wrap ourselves
in tales of warmth
and slip away
from the cold dark.

Jane Mackenzie

Note: Jólabókaflód literally means, 'The Christmas Book Flood' which happens in Iceland each year as people give each other books to read on Christmas Eve.

Figurine

It was Santa who started it;
tears smearing his resin-moulded cheer
as the window wept drear December mist.

Enchanted, Mum had plucked him,
exotic fruit on a charity shop shelf;
he sparkled in her festive tableau.

In the year's wonky gallop towards its end,
he lies atop miscellany and boxes.
Mum had fallen from the ride.

Polly Oliver

Eve of Hope

Hope, hung upon sweet balsam branches
with anticipation of distant dreams.
Love, wrapped in shiny, red ribbons
tucked carefully beneath.
Warmth, surrounding the wonder of it all,
while winter, crystalline, sleeps.

Ann Christine Tabaka

Advent

Advent is here. Its cello-wind notes
close the concert of the year. There are
flurries of snow at night, the tracks of a fox,
imprints of birds that vanished before dawn.
In this new world, the north-wind numbs
to the bone; a crimson-breasted robin plays alone.

This holly wreath is sharp, its leaves
lustrous. In the street, trussed-up walkers
stoop to and from the town's limits
like hunched Lowry figures. Sun sets
polar blue in mid-afternoon.

Matthew M. C. Smith

The New Arrival

In film versions of a Christmas Carol,
that final morning is always ankle-deep,
so I thought snow was a given and wasn't prepared
for five months of November, or the damp
that would coat my lungs like peppermint.

Just once that first year, on Westminster Bridge,
a few flakes blew up the river like ropes of geese
and I waited for one cold petal kiss
to hit my face then headed for the crowds
of night buses in Trafalgar Square.

Caroline Hammond

Since You Asked

What I really want this Christmas is not to forget
A thing, or be forgotten —

Each breath, every sensation,
Every head banging grief or memory,

Gestures of pure love I once gave or received,
All bundled together into one great gold-trimmed

Seam-bursting package.

And I would fall on my knees,
Offer it up to someone, anyone — a child perhaps;

Saying this is from me, this is my life. Take it please.

Lisa McCabe

First-foot

Step out young man, step out
be not here at the bells, on the stroke.
Let mid-night throw off its yoke.
Return with airs of coal
yet bow to pass -
pay your silver at the door
present your dram -
set first-foot fortunes here to last.

Alexandra McCauley

Last Tree

Sitting on the top stair,
streetlight through midnight windows,
I smell the pine we cut, my sisters and I,
a scrawny reject.
"You call that a Christmas tree?" our father asked,
too sick to be drunk, his outrage our point.
We had not expected his tears for the tree,
the last he would have.
Pens and oranges in our stockings, ice on the weathervane,
a starfish instead of a star, a shock of love.

Luanne Rice

Late Shift, 24th December

Waiting for my card to clear, you strike a bored pose.
Your elbow pivots on a tilted hip, a chewed pen twirls

In your free hand., I try to engage, but you have turned away;
gaze lost to the diner's cold, black glass. Beyond, the city

flickers, its hot brown breath of smoke and spirit calling,
while in a distant winter street your family waits, anxious,

resigned, to the first unfurling of strong cobalt wings,
shaking loose the scraps of paper, tinsel and anticipation,

that for seventeen years fired a smile so bright it healed age,
melted time.

Philip Berry

Sol Invictus

At the solstice, the earth tilts
towards the light. A dazzle
of midwinter sun thaws the burn.

Fine fissures spread
and water seeps through
frozen stars where ice grows thin.

Sasha Saben Callaghan

Yuletide

Yule, mischievous winter sprite,
Enters the world
Through a child's eyes.

Forest pine, coal smoke
And winter spice.

Sugar mice with their
String tale.
Fairy kisses, lashes flutter as
Three ships sail closer,
Wearing their new coats of snow.

Dai Fry

Ornaments

The winter we were evicted and you'd been let go,
with no baubles to decorate our Christmas tree,
you sliced up oranges, baked them hard
until the house was scented with orange oil
and they shone like stained glass
among the fairy lights. You made
a gingerbread family with icing smiles,
strapped their bodies to the branches
with satin ribbons. They looked
like people who'd lost their parachutes.

Lucy Whitehead

Christmas Eve

We slipped away from the golden warmth
into the silvery night, looking for winter.
The cat had left a dainty trail for us,
and a robin had scritch-scratched a line
on the white card of the path.

Further up the lane, the mark
of two wings in the snow.
"Owl" we said, wisely, nodding at each other.
knowing an angel
would be more deadly and more beautiful.

Sarah Connor

Christmas Eve

Beyond midnight:
Mum and Dad on the lounge floor,
a last-minute wrapping session;
on the turn of the stairs, I spy them

through oak banisters, picking
at the paint of the skirting board.

They could be happy –

and I would steal away to bed
and yearn in the darkness.

Alan Parry

Colours of Grief (A Winter Requiem)

Falling from a beech tree, straight into winter
a charcoal angel on blank canvas.
Her orange beak, a pickaxe abandoned in the snow.
My gloves - a vermillion blaze
holding her heart; her breath too little,
I too late.

Life slipped into the grass; first fleck of green
we'd seen in weeks. My tears - icicles in feathers.
She loosened her neck with a dignity
that passed all understanding.
Gone.

Tracy Gaughan

Solstice

In the winter sun,
boughs of wild oak
are encumbered by snow;

the stooped shoulders
of my grandmother.

Megha Sood

Solstice Fair

Frost festival fair.
Frozen river in floodlights,
bathing in chill glow.

Ian Richardson

Winter Solstice

Even at noon
the shadows are too long -
dark streamers on a frosted lawn.

Marian Christie

<u>Samhain</u>

The carriageway curves, reaching for clouds
like the contour of a tightly-strung bow.

Edging the horizon, a coin flames
amber, staining the sky scarlet and bronze.

Underneath a curtain of mist, bare trees
wait among leaves of fire and gold.

As day slips into night, the veil between
living and dead thins to a spider-spun shield.

Tonight, like my ancestors before me
I will light a candle and welcome my ghosts.

Nicola Heaney

<u>Christmas Gift 1978</u>

Snow-light through windows
My first-born sleeps on my chest
Flames tick in the grate

Ellie Rees

In Winter's Path

We expect to see no-one
all doors are safely shut at
Mari Lwyd time when we
know, we can be defeated
by a song. The trees bared
show their true shape, soft
dead-wood holds life beneath
our feet. There's little to hide
behind, on walks like these.

Llwybr y Gaeaf.

Ni ddisgwyliwn weld neb
â'r holl ddrysau ar gau yn
ddiogel yn amser y Fari Lwyd
pan fyddwn yn gwybod, gallwn
gael ein trechu gan gân.
Heb ddail, mae coed yn dangos
eu gwirionedd, coed crin sy'n dal
bywyd dan ein traed. Nid oes
llawer i gynnig cuddfan, ar
deithiau fel y rhain.

Ness Owen

Winter-maid (Matariki harvests)

We climb until we hear her. Wailing windfloats the hilltop - finding
    four cold bright ears, tipped keen to the winter-maid's starsong grief

Like the harbour fireworks, some hearts are a conflagration always ready to set off, tonight
    Ra shimmies the black ice, away to the shining arms of another
for Hine-Takurua to forgive – only her strong south currents
    wax a little saltier each year, and there
in the long chill shadows of touchpaper gods, I palm you the foil-skinned planet
    plucked from the coals of the bonfire, left tide-eaten far below

Split deep softsun orange, the sweet kūmara steams, burns fingers
    and eager mouths – a minute more tasted light, and full bellies glow against the dark

Ankh Spice

Advent

A flame sputters,
chokes black smoke
and curls in wisps
to nothing-
Then, a draft;
elemental incarnation.
A small breath
breathes hope.
The flicker leaps
and burns anew.

Jane Mackenzie

Blossoming

The plums leach their heat, shape
brandy into winter's rich wine.

As snow shifts on the Christmas window
we uncork the bottles and jars,

sip the sugar of summer and shiver
as bright light blazes into winter.

Lynn Valentine

Christmas Party

A stranger's hands on my waist,
hot lips brushed the nape of my neck.
Shockingly thrilling, and not unwelcome.
This indelible memory, no identity.

Lesley Williams

Christmas morning

Ma puts more suet on the tree,
right into that crook,
where any bird can spy it.
She doesn't care.
Sparrow, jay, crow, grackle,
all are welcome
on Christmas day
in the morning.

Elizabeth Moura

Boxing Day

You could shatter like a bauble,
prick a heart with the things you said.
But it was magic to be by you,
each afternoon sweet with sugar, a gift.

You died on Boxing Day, oblivious
to ribbons, mince pies, tinsel.
There were the gifts we still hadn't given,
shrouded in splinters, a falling rain of pine needles.

Rae Howells

Christmas Message

She smashed the friendship decades ago
in a careless knock, saw it plummet and splinter.
She swept up its severed continents,
interred them in a cupboard for future repair.
Later she turned over the rough edges,
found too many slivers had been lost.
It will never be whole. But each year,
December flings opens a window.
Each year, as the month ripens,
she writes some words, launches them into air.

Lucy Dixcart

Winter Solstice Incantation

Snapdragon petals, pink and yellow, rose hips, gold
paint chips tossed over my shoulder. Hellebore

and phlox, candles to burn through the long pitch-black.
This spell's being cast at last light and you'll come back

through the mirror's crack like Lazarus from the dead
tonight if I can just find the right words. *Close* and *closed*,

what you were to me and a door slammed shut between
this world and the next. Outside, a wild wind whips

through the trees, whispering its warning—what's done
cannot be undone. Slippery as winter ice, you're gone.

Kim Harvey

<u>Holidays are just small wakes that</u>

remind me of my
mother - god, cinnamon
rolls so sweet. I cannot make
the potatoes right.

More snow here than there and there snow
is ash, or not ash, is buried, or not buried.

Let's sleep in - uncooked, flesh fresh.
Thick pale batter. A wake.

Conyer Clayton

<u>Moth</u>

You arrived on the Solstice, settled in a corner,
with wings tucked in, a neat, tiny fan
and your furred head, the mink of an autumn thistle.
The flicker of the candle's wick danced
to the crackle and hiss of log sap spit.

In dawn light of the turning earth
I found you, still, on the window sill,
your papery wing residue
a farewell on my fingers

Lorraine Carey

The Edges

Shells like leather, left too long
by the remains of a fire, tumble from
the edges of great-grandmother's cut-glass dish,
scatter across the faded, crimson tablecloth
as voices tire, as aging hands slow,
picking from this day, with care, the last
bits of the plumpest walnuts, chestnuts, cashews.

Tomorrow, we'll wash the gold-trimmed china, then
pack it all away awaiting the promise of next year.

A. A. Parr

Winter, maybe

an unquiet term,
autumn's crimson giving ground
in midwinter thaw

the waters came on
twins under shelter, sight of snow,
the veining maple, lips skeletal
against white cover

this claret drained for lack of light
what it could be to the boar-bile bones
a twinning brother, his nobody hand prelapsed, precise -

the stigmata of sulfur, empty these words
hand in hand a mother-ringed womb

the moment we let go

Erin Russell

Throwing Shade

Dumbstruck by January,
just a few tepid hours of daylight,
the yews still cast their shadows

    though nothing else does…

Late afternoon, the lights switched on and yet
the yews still throw shade at me

    like green moonlight.

I'll keep it as a secret insult –
my silent communion with trees.

Ellie Rees

The Star in the East

Wolf-moon-light
blooms in the dawn-dusk sky

Trees with bare-black-boughs
guide the way

Beyond the horizon, hidden,
a star looms

ox-blood-bright

Iris Anne Lewis

End of the day

Friday. Time passes. The black crow
cloaked by shadow –
slump into armchairs, stoke the coals.

Huddled, the flickering stops
abruptly, test card, hum, listen.

It whistles out there. Drift
leaves, drizzle, nothing.

Patrick Williamson

Frost

Concrete is crystalline
cold light of halogen,
steel through night
procession of chrome

Smooth arc of moon
at the end of breath
planets bright, pure light
between rise of star-sun
and down of dusk
with all motion
encircling Polaris

Matthew M. C. Smith

ON THE SECOND DAY OF CHRISTMAS MY TRUE LOVE GAVE TO ME TWO TURTLE DOVES

Contributors

Artist

Artist Emma Bissonnet grew up in Norfolk, studied Art in Sheffield & Swansea, and gained a City & Guilds in Printmaking on Gower. She has worked in conservation & gardening across Wales. Her inspiration comes from a deep love of nature. Emma's prints feature Welsh landscapes, wildlife and folklore. etsy.com/uk/shop/EmmaBissonnetDesigns facebook.com/EmmaBissonnetDesigns instagram.com/emmabissonnetdesigns Twitter: @EmmaBissonnet pinterest.co.uk/emmabissonnetdesigns

Poets

Catherine Fisher is a poet and writer for children and young adults. Her latest collection is *The Bramble King* (Seren, 2019) and her most recent novel The Midnight Swan (2020). She is a past winner of the Cardiff International Poetry Competition and was the first Young People's Laureate for Wales.

Julian Brasington lives in North West Wales. His poems have appeared most recently in *Ink Sweat and Tears*, *Morning Star*, and *Dust*, and are forthcoming in *Stand* and *Channel*.

Pax Morrigan is on a quest for imagination and loves playing with words. Twitter: @paxmorrigan www.paxmorrigan.com

Boris Simonovski is a second year undergraduate student in the Faculty of Philology, Blazhe Koneski, in Skopje, Macedonia, where he studies English Language and Literature. A number of his poems are published in the anthologies *Oceans of Emotions* and *Oriental Prism 3*.

Leela Soma was born in Madras/Chennai, India and now lives in Glasgow. Her poems and short stories have been published in a number of anthologies, publications. She has published two novels and two collections of poetry. She has served on the Scottish Writer's Centre Committee and is now in East Dunbartonshire Arts & Culture Committee. Some of her work reflects her dual heritage of India and Scotland.

Ronnie Smith is 61, comes originally from Glasgow, has travelled widely, lives in south west France and has published stories and articles in the U.K., France, Romania and Australia. He came late to writing poetry, having been unable to find a voice until recently, but better late than never.

Rafferty Wolfe is a photographer and poet from Whitby in North Yorkshire. She frequently works with themes of religion, nature and personal and cultural displacement, and seeks the establishment of a new contemporary Gothic poetry.

Laura Wainwright is from Newport, South Wales. Her poetry has been published, or is forthcoming, in *Black Bough Poetry*, *Burning House Press*, *Wales Haiku Journal*, *Picaroon Poetry*, *Animal Heart Press* and *Lucent Dreaming*. Twitter: @wainwrightlj

Guinevere Clark lives in Swansea, Wales. She is studying for a PhD in Creative Writing, forming a new collection based on maternity, single parenting and gender inequality. Her first book is 'Fresh Fruit & Screams', *Bluechrome Press* (2006). Recent poems have appeared in: *Minerva Rising*, *The A3* and *Atlanta Reviews*, *Black Bough Poetry*, *Magma*. She was commended in *Ambit's* 2020 Poetry Competition. www.guinevereclark.com

Ryan Norman is a writer from New York living in the Hudson Valley. Inspired by the landscape, he writes what he feels. His work has appeared in *From Whispers to Roars*, *Vamp Cat Magazine*, *Black Bough Poetry*, *Storgy Magazine* and elsewhere. You can find him on Twitter @RyanMGNorman

George Neame is a publisher from London whose poems have previously appeared in *the moth*, *Acumen*, *Antiphon* and *Ink, Sweat & Tears*. In his spare time he enjoys pub quizzes, long walks, and dangerously strong coffee.

Marcelle Newbold loves poetry as a way of exploring inner digressions, capturing the unexceptional every day. A member of The Dipping Pool writing group, she lives in Cardiff, Wales, where she trained as an architect. Twitter: @marcellenewbold

Matthew M. C. Smith is a 'Best of the Net' - nominated poet from Swansea, Wales. His work is in *The Lonely Crowd*, *Barren Magazine*, *Icefloe Press* and *Seventh Quarry Press*. He is the editor of Black Bough poetry. Twitter: @MatthewMCSmith

Preston Smith is an MA candidate in Rhetoric & Writing at Wright State University. He has interned with *Mid-American Review* and worked as the Managing Editor of *Prairie Margins*. He can be found on Twitter (and Instagram!) @psm_writes, tweeting about his cats, Helios and Misty, and his love for fairy tales. He has poems published in *Black Bough Poetry*, *Brave Voices Magazine*, *Catfish Creek*, *Nightingale & Sparrow*, and *Pink Plastic House a tiny journal*, among others.

E. Samples lives in Indiana with her family of L.P. (human), Gypsy (queen cat), Dot (calico-fox cat), Black & White (beautiful nuisance cat), & Yoshi (smallest of dogs). For Christmas, she would very much like to see a ghost. Twitter: @emilysamples

Paul Brookes is a shop asst. who lives in Wombwell. His recent chapbooks include *Please Take Change* (Cyberwit.net, 2018), *Stubborn Sod*, (*Alien Buddha Press*, 2019) and *As Folk Over Yonder* (*Afterworld Books*, 2019). He edits The Wombwell Rainbow Interviews.

Carole Bromley is a York poet and the 2019 Hamish Canham winner. Fourth collection is *The Peregrine Falcons of York Minster*, from *Valley Press* 2020

Polly Oliver hails from Cornwall and lives in Swansea. She's been writing poetry on and off for years, mainly reading it at open mic nights across the city and enjoys hearing the work of other local poets and spoken word artists. Her poems have been published in *Black Bough*, Spillwords.com and on her blog 'RocksandBones – Poems from the Celtic Fringes'.

Ann Christine Tabaka was nominated for the 2017 Pushcart Prize in Poetry, has been internationally published, and won poetry awards from numerous publications. She is the author of 9 poetry books. Christine lives in Delaware, USA. She loves gardening and cooking. Chris lives with her husband and three cats.

Caroline Hammond is a founding member of the LetterPress Poetry Group. Her poems have appeared in *Under The Radar* and *Finished Creatures* magazines. Her adopted city, London, often features in her poetry. Twitter: @carolinehpoet1

Merril D. Smith is a historian and poet. She's written non-fiction books and had poetry published here and there. She likes the moon. Website and blog at www.merrildsmith.com, Twitter: @merril_mds, and Instagram at mdsmithnj.

Tracy Gaughan is a Galway based writer. Her work has appeared in *Live Encounters*, *Boyne Berries*, *Headstuff* and others. She is the IRL/UK poetry editor at *The Blue Nib Magazine*.

Karen Hodgson Pryce lives in Aviemore, Scotland. Her poetry is found in *Northwords Now*, *Butcher's Dog*, *Black Bough Poetry*, *Lighthouse (Issue 21)*, *The Poets' Republic* and *Ink, Sweat & Tears*. She won 3rd Prize in Café Writers Open Poetry Competition 2019.

Gaynor Beesley is a poet/writer currently based in the West Midlands. She has been placed and shortlisted in several competitions including The Creative Future Writers' Awards 2019. Her poems have featured in anthologies published by *Write out Loud* with short stories appearing in *Ad Hoc Fiction* and on The Arts Foundry website.

Jane Mackenzie lives in Scotland and loves to write haiku and observational poetry. She also writes for children and will have a haiku published in a children's anthology on insects early next year. Twitter: @jpmackwriter,

Lisa McCabe lives in Lahave, Nova Scotia. She has published poems in *The Sewanee Review*, *HCE Review*, *Nonbinary Review*, *Better Than Starbucks*, *Limestone Review*, among other print and online journals. She works in the field of software translation.

Alexandra McCauley lives in the Scottish Borders with her husband and two black Labradors.

Luanne Rice is the New York Times bestselling author of 33 novels that have been translated into 24 languages. She received the 2014 Connecticut Governor's Arts Award for excellence and lifetime achievement as a literary artist. Her latest book is *The Shadow Box*.

Philip Berry's poems have appeared in *Lucent Dreaming*, *Lunate Fiction*, *Bunbury Magazine*, *Easy Street* and *Picaroon* among others. He lives in London and works as a doctor. His work can explored at www.philberrycreative.wordpress.com Twitter: @philaberry

Sasha Saben Callaghan is a disabled writer and digital artist, living on the Forth estuary. She was a winner of the 2016 'A Public Space' Emerging Writer Fellowship and the 2019 Pen to Paper Awards. Her illustrations have featured in three national art shows during 2019. Twitter: @SabenCallaghan Insta: Sasha Saben

Dai Fry is from Swansea. He now lives in Weymouth. His poems have been published in *Black Bough Poetry* and *Re-side*. He has recently discovered the joy of painting with words. Twitter: @thnargg seekingthedarklight.co.uk

Lucy Whitehead has poetry in *Amethyst Review, Anti-Heroin Chic, Barren Magazine, Burning House Press, Collective Unrest, Electric Moon Magazine, Ghost City Review, Mookychick Magazine, Neon Mariposa Magazine, Pussy Magic, Re-side, Twist in Time Magazine*. Twitter @blueirispoetry.

Sarah Connor lives in the deep southwest and has worked with children with mental health difficulties, grows apples and writes poetry. Twitter: @sacosw fmmewritespoems.wordpress.com

Alan Parry is a poet, playwright and poetry editor from Merseyside, England. He is an English Literature graduate and English teacher. Alan enjoys gritty realism, open ends, miniature schnauzers and 60s girl groups. He has previously had work published by *Dream Noir, Porridge Magazine, Black Bough* Poems and others. He cites Alan Bennett, Stan Barstow and James Joyce as inspiration. His debut poetry collection, *Neon Ghosts* is available from www.thebrokenspine.co.uk/shop

Megha Sood is an editor at *Mookychick* (UK) and *Cross Tree Press* (US). Works featured in *Statorec, Piker, Visitant Lit, Dime Show Review,* etc. Works featured/upcoming in 50 anthologies by US, UK, and 11 Canadian presses. State-level NJ Poetry Winner 2018/19/20. Spring Mahogany National Level Winner 2020.

Ian Richardson was Overall Winner in the Scottish Borders 'Waverley Lines' poetry competition in 2015. In November 2016, he received the Anstruther Writing Award. His work has appeared in various poetry publications and spoken word podcasts. Twitter: @IanRich10652022

Marian Christie reads and writes poetry, looks at the stars, puzzles over the laws of physics and listens to birdsong.
www.marianchristiepoetry.net
Twitter: @marian_v_o.

Nicola Heaney is a Derry-born, Bristol-based poet. Her work has been shortlisted for the Bridport Prize and appeared in publications such as *The North* magazine, *Honest Ulsterman* and *Riggwelter*.

Ellie Rees's first collection of poetry is to be published by *Hedgehog Press* in 2021. Twitter: @ellierees23

Ness Owen is from Ynys Mon. Her poems have been published in journals and anthologies including in *Poetry Wales, Red Poets, Mslexia, Arachne Press, Mother's Milk Books* and *Three Drops Press*. Her collection *Mamiaith* (Mother-tongue) is published with *Arachne Press*. Twitter: @Ness_Owen

Ankh Spice is a sea-obsessed poet from Aotearoa (NZ), whose poetry appears in a number of international publications. He truly believes that narrative and kindness create change, and you'll find him doing his best to prove it Twitter: @SeaGoatScreams
or @AnkhSpiceSeaGoatScreamsPoetry on Facebook.

Lynn Valentine lives on the Black Isle with husband and Labradors. She is currently being mentored by *Cinnamon Press* after winning a place on their mentoring scheme. Her work appears in places such as the Scottish Poetry Library archive, *Northwords Now* and *Atrium*. She hopes to give birth to a pamphlet soon .

Lesley Williams lives in Swansea. After a long career in Social Services, early retirement gave her the opportunity to attend a variety of writing courses run by the University. She has performed her work locally as a member of the Garage Players and continues to meet monthly with a small group of Swansea poets. Lesley can be found on Facebook and on Twitter: @Lesley60510918

Elizabeth Moura lives in a converted factory and works with elders. She has had poetry, flash fiction or photographs published in several online and print publications. She can be reached on Twitter: @mourapoet Insta: mourathepoet.

Rae Howells is a poet and journalist from Swansea. She has won the Rialto Nature and Place and Welsh International poetry competitions and been published in journals including *Rialto*, *Poetry Wales*, *Magma*, *Acumen*, *Envoi*, *New Welsh Review* and *Poetry Ireland*. Her pamphlet, *Bloom & Bones*, written collaboratively with Jean James, is published by *Hedgehog Press*. Twitter: @raehowells

Lucy Dixcart lives in rural Kent with her family. Her poems have appeared in *Acumen*, *Eye Flash Poetry* and *Riggwelter*, as well as in *Pale Fire*, an anthology of lunar poetry by *The Frogmore Press*. She has an MA in Creative Writing from Bath Spa University. Twitter: @lucydixcart

Kim Harvey is a San Francisco Bay Area poet and Associate Editor of *Palette Poetry*. Her work has appeared in *The Comstock Review*, *Rattle*, *Radar*, *Barren Magazine*, *Typishly*, *Poets Reading the News*, and elsewhere. Twitter: @kimharveypoet. Insta: @luna_jack. www.kimharvey.net

Conyer Clayton is an Ottawa-based writer, musician, editor, and gymnastics coach. She has 7 chapbooks, 2 albums, and won The Capilano Review's 2019 Robin Blaser Poetry Prize. Her debut full-length collection is *We Shed Our Skin Like Dynamite* (2020, *Guernica Editions*). Stay updated on her endeavours at conyerclayton.com

Lorraine Carey's poems have appeared in *Prole*, *Smithereens*, *Orbis*, *Constellate*, *Poetry Birmingham Literary Journal*, *Poetry Ireland Review* and *Abridged*. Her art and photography have also featured in various journals. Her debut collection is *From Doll House Windows* (*Revival Press*).

A. A. Parr is a Canadian writer, artist and entrepreneur with a Spec Honours BFA from York University. She writes a weekly series of poetry for strangers on Channillo.com* and her debut chapbook, *What Lasts Beyond the Burning* is forthcoming from *Nightingale & Sparrow Press* in 2020. Twitter: @ifitfeelswrite .

Erin Russell is a writer from Calgary living in Amsterdam. Winner of the 2019 Patricia Goedicke Prize for Poetry and the University of Toronto's Wycliffe College Poetry Award, her work has appeared or is forthcoming in *CutBank*, *Burning House*, *Train*, *Talking About Strawberries*, *Time Out*, and *The Holland Times*, a.o., and has been translated into French and Chinese. She lectures at Amsterdam University College. Twitter: @etcall

Iris Anne Lewis writes poetry and short stories. Her work has been featured at the Cheltenham Literary Festival and the Bradford on Avon Arts Festival. She has been successful in local and national competitions and is published in magazines and anthologies. Twitter: @IrisAnneLewis

Patrick Williamson - latest collections are *Traversi*, *Beneficato*, *Nel Santuario* (English-Italian, Samuele Editore), *Gifted* (Corrupt Press). Editor and translator of *The Parley Tree, An Anthology of Poets from French-speaking Africa and the Arab World* (*Arc Publications*), founder member of transnational agency Linguafranca.

OUT NOW on Amazon KDP

Deep Time volume 1

Deep Time volume 2

"*Underland* acted merely as that entrance-point […] the writers and artists gathered here have carried out their own fathomings and explorations, and the result is a collection of work that feels both contemporary and mythic, urgent and ancient."

Robert Macfarlane

Printed in Great Britain
by Amazon